WALSINGHAM

in Times Past

Rev. Peter Rollings S.M.

£2·00

The Walsingham Picture, a painting by Alan Sorrell, from the conference room at the Roman Catholic Hostel, which depicts Our Lady of Walsingham in the community of the great saints of England — Edward, Alban, Bede, Aidan, Julian of Norwich, Thomas of Canterbury, Thomas More ...... In the background can be seen the Saxon Holy House, the remaining arch of the Priory Church and the Slipper Chapel.

Published by Countryside Publications Limited, School Lane, Brinscall, Chorley, Lancashire.
Text © Rev. Peter Rollings. SM. 981
Printed by: Tamley-Reed Limited.
ISBN 0 86157 046 4

Introduction

Walsingham is a small village lying in the valley of the River Stiffkey in north west Norfolk, about five miles from the coast. Its fine half-timbered houses and picturesque Common Place make it a tourist attraction like so many of our old English villages and yet Walsingham lays claim to an international reputation and boasts the title "England's Nazareth". Why should this be so?

Walsingham's importance comes from the fact that here, in 1061, the Lady Richeldis de Faverche, widow of the Lord of the Manor of Walsingham, was inspired to build a small house in wood, wattle and daub. It was to serve as a reminder of the house in Nazareth where, according to Saint Luke's Gospel, the Archangel Gabriel came to Mary with God's request that she should be the mother of his Son.

The earliest written account of Richeldis' inspiration is in a 15th century ballad published by Richard Pynson and now in the Bodlian Library, Oxford. This relates how Richeldis desired to do some work for God and was led in spirit to the Holy Land by Our Lady and there shown the Holy House of Jesus, Mary and Joseph. Richeldis was told to note its measurements and build one like it in Walsingham "unto my laud and singular honour",

Our Lady said, "and all who me seek there shall find succour."

This small house became the focus of a devotion which has continued to this day. In 1153 a Priory of Augustinian Canons was founded to care for the Shrine. In time, beside the Holy House they built a great Priory Church (of which only the perpendicular-style east window remains). The Holy House itself was so sacred that it was left unaltered although protected by a small chapel.

The fame of Walsingham, strengthened by the many accounts of favours received there, spread rapidly. By the time of the destruction of the Holy House in 1538 every King of England from Henry III to Henry VIII had come on pilgrimage and so many lesser folk that the roads to Walsingham were reputed to resemble the Milky Way which then became known as the Walsingham Way. Holinshed, the Elizabethan chronicler, places the road from London to Walsingham in the first place among the roads of England. It was held to be the duty of every Englishman to visit Our Lady of Walsingham at least once in his life.

As a consequence, the tiny hamlet of Walsingham grew to be an important market town and the centre of local administration. Until a few years ago when it was swallowed by the North Norfolk District Council, based at Cromer, the local authority showed traces of this in its name — Walsingham Rural District Council — and until recently there was a regular court held in the Common Place where the Court House is now preserved as a museum.

The development of Walsingham was so complete that it is said the actual street pattern was made to reflect that of Nazareth so that in all respects this was truly England's Nazareth.

At the Reformation, Walsingham was one of the four major shrines of Christendom ranking with Jerusalem, Rome and Compostella. It was not surprising, then, that the eyes of the reformers were immediately upon the Shrine and the Priory became one of the first religious houses to surrender to the King in 1536. In 1538 the Shrine was dismantled by the King's commissioners, the Holy House was razed to the ground, the revered statue was taken to Chelsea for burning and those who spoke out against the changes were ruthlessly executed before their fellow villagers.

But, as Gamaliel had prophesied in the Acts of the Apostles, "if this plan or this undertaking is of men it will fail; but if it is of God, you will not be able to overthrow them." (Acts 5:38f) And so the devotion of Walsingham continued through penal times. There is evidence that, even when the Catholic Church in England was at its lowest ebb, there were strangers who would annoy the tenant of the cottage built on to the the Slipper Chapel outside Walsingham by asking to enter his barn (the chapel) where they would kneel and pray.

The Slipper Chapel, built in the 14th century and said to be one of the finest examples of a decorated west front in England, was the last of the station chapels which marked the route to Walsingham. It was to play a decisive role in the restoration of the Shrine. For, when Charlotte Boyd rescued the chapel from use as a barn in the 1890s, it once more became a focus of devotion and, in 1897, the first publicly organised pilgrimage of modern times came and the flood gates were once more opened.

Although Walsingham is part of our nation's heritage and has a venerable history, it is not a museum-piece. Today it is a living Shrine, as vibrant as ever it was, a place where the children of God, whatever their creed, grow together as his family under the protection of their Mother.

Peter Rollings S.M. 1981

The trail to Walsingham had many starting-points. From simple dwellings all over England men and women of every kind set off to seek the aid of the Mother of God in Walsingham. Many also began their journey from homes which were more elaborate than that of the Holy Family and from this house, Barsham Manor, two miles from Walsingham, Henry VIII began to walk in his bare feet to Our Lady's Shrine. The house is said to be one of the finest examples of a Tudor brick building in England.
(Photo: Greenhoe Press)

On their journey the pilgrims' way was marked by wayside crosses and chapels where they would stop to rest and pray. This is the Slipper Chapel at Houghton St. Giles pictured in 1893. (Are these some of the earliest pilgrims?). For centuries this was the last of the stopping places on the route to Walsingham. The name may come from the custom of pilgrims removing their shoes here before entering the Holy Land of Walsingham itself. It is actually dedicated to St. Catherine of Alexandria, the patroness of pilgrims, and is so orientated that the sun rises directly behind the altar on November 25, her feast day. After the Dissolution of the Monasteries it was used as a Poor House, a barn and a cow shed. But, even through penal days, pilgrims continued to pray here.

The Slipper Chapel was built in the middle of the 14th century and has been described as one of the finest examples of a decorated west front in England. Architectural details suggest that it may have been the work of Alan of Walsingham who was responsible for the lantern tower of Ely Cathedral. This photograph is dated 1891.

Above right: The chapel was rescued from dereliction by the action of Miss Charlotte Boyd, an Anglican looking for somewhere to house a community of nuns. Charlotte restored the chapel at her own expense and this photograph, probably taken in 1896, shows the restoration work in progress.

Below right: This photograph, also taken during the restoration work in about 1896, shows the Slipper Chapel being freed from the cottages and outbuildings which had gradually become attached to it. Most of the building, including the roof timbers, is still the original work of the 14th century.

Right: Charlotte Pearson Boyd, who restored the Slipper Chapel to religious use, was an Anglican and a great benefactoress of religious houses. She ran her own orphanage in Kilburn. Whilst the Slipper Chapel was under restoration she was received into the Catholic Church and she then gave the chapel to the monks of Downside Abbey. She died in London on April 3 1906. (Photo: Greenhoe Press)

Left: Miss Boyd's great wish was to see the Slipper Chapel as a shrine of Our Lady at Walsingham. But the Catholic centre for Walsingham at that time was at King's Lynn and it was there in 1897 that the Shrine of Our Lady of Walsingham was officially restored in the Church of the Annunciation, London Road, where it can be visited today. Unfortunately the shrine was modelled on the younger Italian Shrine of Loreto rather than on the ancient Holy House of Walsingham.

In 1338, in order to help care for the increasing number of pilgrims coming to the Shrine, the Franciscans came to Walsingham and established this Friary. This began a long tradition of Franciscan involvement in the care of pilgrims which has continued to the present day. This postcard was sent from Walsingham on June 6 1908 and informs the recipient that a case of eggs has just been despatched to her in London by the same train ! Walsingham's station — a victim of Dr. Beeching's axe — is now a Russian Orthodox church.

Left: As Walsingham's fame spread so the village developed and its centre moved from around the Parish Church of All Saints to the area of the Shrine. The Common Place, pictured here, became a focal point. In the picture can be seen the Conduit House which had the three-fold function of village pump, lock-up and beacon. It is said that on one occasion Parliament, following the King on his progress around the country, met here.
(Photo: Greenhoe Press)

Inns developed around the Common Place and along the High Street beside the Priory gate to cater for the pilgrims. Some of these half-timbered buildings have returned to their original use, others are now shops or houses. This view of the High Street from the Common Place was taken in the 1930s. (Photo: C.F.)

Another scene from the 1930s. The shop on the corner of the High Street and the Common Place was at this time a saddlers and harnessmakers and the proprietor, Mr. A. Newton, can be seen in the doorway working on a farm saddle.
(Photo: C.F.)

Walsingham's long summer of popularity was to become her winter of neglect in 1583 when the King's commissioners destroyed the Shrine and began the process of despoilation which resulted in this lone arch, once the great east window, being all that remains of the Priory church which was built beside the Holy House.

In Walsingham's desolation the twin wells which had been associated with the origin of the Shrine and which had played their part in many favours and answers to prayer were reduced to being "wishing wells" and were visited more by the curious than the faithful.

Above right: But winter was to give way to spring once more when, in 1921, the Vicar of Walsingham, Father Alfred Hope Patten, restored the Shrine of Our Lady of Walsingham in the 15th century parish church of St. Mary and All Saints. Again the story of the Shrine's development was repeated and a new church had to be built in 1931 to house the Shrine. On October 15 1931 the Shrine was translated to the new church and here we see the beginning of the translation procession.

Below right: ". . . I went with the throng, and led them in procession to the house of God, with glad shouts and songs of thanksgiving, a multitude keeping festival." (Ps. 42)

Right: The procession, through flag-decked streets, enters the Common Place on its way to the new Shrine Church.

Left: Anglican priests, tapers in hand, escort the statue to its new home.

Right: "You are the highest honour of our race !" — The statue of Our Lady of Walsingham is borne by deacons in the translation procession. In the background is the former Swan Inn, a medieval hostelry. Today it is the convent of the Marist Sisters who work at the Catholic Shrine.

Left: The singing of the Magnificat outside the Shrine Church on the day of the translation. "My soul magnifies the Lord... For behold all generations will call me blessed; for he who is mighty has done great things for me ...." (Lk.1.)

Almost 400 years after the destruction of Richeldis' shrine, a new Holy House is erected in Walsingham. Here we see the statue enthroned in the Anglican Shrine.

Above right: One of Father Hope Patten's great supporters in restoring the Shrine was Bishop O'Rourke who became Rector of Blakeney. He presided over the translation and is pictured here with Father Hope Patten on the right.

Below right: In the 1930s it seemed in Walsingham that the harvest had finally come and the fruits of much labour were being reaped both in the Anglican and Roman Catholic churches. This glimpse of the harvest near Walsingham was taken, symbolically, on August 19 1934 when the Slipper Chapel was inaugurated — with the approval of the Pope — as the National Shrine of Our Lady in England.

On the day of the inauguration the tiny restored Slipper Chapel was surrounded by tens of thousands of pilgrims who were led by Cardinal Bourne.

Once again the roads to Walsingham were thronged with pilgrims as they were from 1061 to 1538 — but this time their mode of travel was very different !

The Law and the Prophets !

As the Pynson ballad relates: "the lame, the halt, the vexed, the blind ....." all gather at Our Lady's feet. These pilgrims are waiting for the start of the Blessed Sacrament procession.

These pilgrims are from Leicester and they are singing the Rosary on their way to the pilgrimage.

Bishops, come to honour God in his Mother on this historic day as did their forefathers in times past.

But what our forefathers never had was a police escort on a motorcycle like this one who crosses the River Stiffkey ahead of the pilgrimage.

The last Cardinal to visit Walsingham before the Reformation was Wolsey who came as a sick man to seek a cure. By coincidence the next Cardinal — Cardinal Bourne — was also a sick man. He had made a vow to lead this pilgrimage and he kept his word by following the Blessed Sacrament in his car, driven by his secretary.

Right: The first photograph of the re-established Catholic Shrine was taken on the day of its inauguration by the donor, Miss Hilda Carey, whose own note on the back of the photograph relates that it was given to the Slipper Chapel in memory of her brother, Lieutenant Launcelot Carey, who fell in action on July 21 1916.

Left: A pilgrimage in procession through Friday Market on its way to the Slipper Chapel in 1935. On the right is Mr. George Back's grocery shop. The house in the background had just been bought and was in use as St. Aelred's Guest House, a use it maintained for a very short while before becoming the Franciscan Friary for about 10 years and, in latter years, the Pilgrim Bureau and Hostel. (Picture and caption: C. F.)

In ancient times the only way to Walsingham was on foot but at the same time the pilgrimage journey provided a deep insight into the mystery of the Pilgrim People of God on their way to the heavenly Jerusalem. Many have found walking pilgrimages a fruitful experience like these who made the first walking pilgrimage of modern times. They are shown making a stop at the pump at West Wratting in July 1935. (Photo: C.F.)

Pilgrimages have never been purely prayer and penance. Groups of pilgrims have always made the most of each others' company and, centuries ago, permission was granted for the Priory at Walsingham to hold a number of fairs in the village. This picture, taken in 1935, shows what was probably the last Corpus Christi fair in the Common Place.
(Photo: C.F.)

There was no merriment, however, when the Dissolution of the Monasteries came to Walsingham. Two local men, Nicholas Mileham (the sub-prior of the monastery) and George Guisborough (a layman) spoke out against the changes and were hanged, drawn and quartered in what is still known in Walsingham as the Martyrs' Field. The night before their execution they were reputedly kept in the cellar of the house now known as the Martyrs' House opposite the Priory gate. This photograph of the cellar was taken on November 2 1935 and at the time the instruments in the niche were said to have been used in torturing the martyrs. The house now belongs to the Sue Ryder Foundation. (Photo: C.F.)

After the destruction of the Shrine an old woman of Wells-next-the-Sea claimed favours through the intercession of Our Lady of Walsingham. She was arrested and placed in the stocks where the boys of Walsingham threw snowballs at her. The complaint was made that "the said image is not yet out of some of their heads." Indeed the memory of Our Lady of Walsingham has continued to the present day. These women came on the first overnight pilgrimage to the Catholic Shrine in modern times. They stayed at Wells-next-the-Sea and are pictured here on the feast of the Annunciation 1936 at the holy wells in the Abbey grounds. (Photo: C.F.)

The road to Walsing-
ham takes many dif-
ferent forms, both
physically as well as
spiritually, for many
pilgrims. These pil-
grims came by train
(at that time the Slip-
per Chapel had its
own Halt) and are
greeted by Father Br-
uno Scott James, the
Priest-Custodian of
the Catholic Shrine.
(Photo: C.F.)

The welcome for pilgrims in former days was at the gateway to the Priory and Shrine, pictured here in 1938, 400 years after the gates were finally closed to pilgrims. (Photo: C.F.)

High Street, Walsingham, in about 1938. The Flemish-style gable of the house in the centre of the picture reflects East Anglia's connections with the Low Countries in the wool trade. (Photo: C.F.)

The Oxford Stores, one of the oldest buildings in Walsingham, was once a medieval hostelry and thrives as such today. This photograph was taken at Christmas time in about 1938. (Photo: C.F.)

The past and the present were quite definitely joined after a 400 year break when, on the anniversary of the destruction of the Shrine in 1538, this crowd of pilgrims to the Shrine of Our Lady in 1938 gathered in the Common Place to sing the Credo by torchlight.

(Photo: C.F.)

When the Rev. B. Scott James said Mass in the Spanish front line, the Marquess de Villada gave him his red beret to hang before the Shrine of Our Lady of Walsingham, in the Slipper Chapel in thanksgiving for his having served through the Spanish campaign unscathed. The picture shows Father James carrying out the Marquess' bidding on March 25 1939. (Picture and Caption : C.F.)

One of the most unusual and dramatic pilgrimages to Walsingham was the cross-carrying pilgrimage in 1948 which took place as an act of reparation after the war and as a prayer for peace. The 14 oak crosses were carried from all parts of England and on July 15 were borne into the village for a service at the site of the original Shrine.
(Photo: Greenhoe Press)

Cardinal Griffin speaks to the congregation at the conclusion of the cross-carrying pilgrimage. The priest beside him is Derek Worlock, now Archbishop of Liverpool. The 14th cross carried by the group in the centre of the picture came from Middlesbrough and travelled the longest distance of the 14. After this ceremony the crosses were erected as a Way of the Cross at the Slipper Chapel where they remain today.

Many pilgrims see Walsingham as a sort of "Brigadoon" which disappears as soon as they leave. This photograph, taken in 1951, shows that the village still goes on even when the streets are not thronged with pilgrims. This is the south end of the village looking up the High Street before the removal of the telegraph poles and, left, into Friday Market before the demolition of the building next to the Black Lion to make way for the Catholic church. (Photo: C.F.)

After the restoration of the Catholic Shrine the Catholic population of Walsingham grew and in 1951 they opened their first church. Here we see the Franciscan Friars helping to demolish a cottage in Friday Market to make way for it. (Photo: C.F.)

In 1950 the belief that, at the end of her earthly life, Mary was assumed body and soul into heaven was defined as dogma. The east window of the Slipper Chapel, shown here, commemorates the Assumption. The central panel was blessed on Assumption Sunday 1953 and the work finished in September that year. It was the last work of the artist, Geoffrey Webb, who died shortly after. (Photo: Greenhoe Press)

During World War Two Walsingham was in a restricted zone. Pilgrimages were interrupted for a while, with the exception of those organised by servicemen, particularly from the United States Air Force, who have retained a special link with Walsingham. These airmen from nearby Sculthorpe are pictured here as a guard of honour for Cardinal Griffin who is arriving at the Priory gate for the annual pilgrimage of the Union of Catholic Mothers in July 1953.

The year 1954 was another milestone in Walsingham's history. In this year, generally observed as a Marian Year, a newly-carved statue of Our Lady of Walsingham was crowned at the site of the original Shrine on behalf of the Pope by Archbishop O'Hara, the Apostolic Delegate. An unusual touch was the placing of two doves at the feet of the statue where they remained throughout the procession along the Holy Mile until the statue was enthroned in the Slipper Chapel where it is a focus for devotion today.
(Picture: Pathe News)

As Mary stood beneath the cross of her Son as he offered himself in sacrifice, so her children are brought by her to that same sacrifice in Walsingham. Here for the first time, at the National Pilgrimage in 1958, we notice sick pilgrims in a group which reflects the diversity of vocations to the service of God and yet a common ideal. (Photo: C.F.)

Acknowledgements

Thanks must be given to those who have taken pains to build up the photographic archives from which these pictures have been taken and especially to Mr. Claude Fisher, who took many of the photographs reproduced here. I am also indebted to Claude and to Father Roland Connelly S.M. for much of the information and for fostering my regard for Walsingham's great past.

Peter Rollings S.M.

COUNTRYSIDE PUBLICATIONS LIMITED

• • • • • • • CURRENT BOOK AND PRICE LIST

* **LARGE FORMAT (A4) BOOKS 'IN TIMES PAST' SERIES**

☐ STOCKTON (ISBN 0 86157 015 4: 44 pps; 62 photographs); £1.50
☐ LANCASTER & MORECAMBE (ISBN 0 86157 004 9: 40 pps; 74 photographs): £1.65
☐ STRETFORD (ISBN 0 86157 024 3: 40 pps; 62 photographs): £1.60
☐ GATESHEAD (ISBN 0 86157 026 X: 48 pps; 71 photographs): £1.80

* **SMALL FORMAT (A5) BOOKS 'IN TIMES PAST' SERIES**

☐ WORKSOP (ISBN 0 86157 023 5: 48 pps; 59 photographs): £1.20
☐ HEATHROW & DISTRICT (ISBN 0 86157 014 6: 64 pps; 71 photographs): £1.50
☐ BOOTLE (ISBN 0 86157 022 7: 40 pps; 41 photographs): £1.20
☐ LYTHAM ST. ANNE'S (ISBN 0 86157 010 3: 56 pps; 64 photographs): £1.25
☐ SUTTON IN ASHFIELD (ISBN 0 86157 006 5: 48 pps; 56 photographs): £1.00
☐ ULVERSTON (ISBN 0 86157 020 0: 48 pps; 54 photographs): £1.20
☐ THIRSK PAST AND PRESENT (ISBN 0 86157 029 4: 48 pps; 49 photographs): £1.45

* **SMALL FORMAT (A5) SPECIALIZED RECIPE BOOKS**

☐ LANCASHIRE RECIPES OLD & NEW (ISBN 0 86157 018 9: 48 pps; 85 recipes; 19 vintage illustrations): £1.00
☐ LAKELAND RECIPES OLD & NEW (ISBN 0 86157 008 1: 80 pps; 123 recipes; 21 vintage illustrations): £1.50
☐ GLOUCESTERSHIRE RECIPES OLD & NEW (ISBN 0 86157 013 8: 48 pps; 100 recipes; 15 vintage illustrations): £1.00
☐ GAME COOKERY – SOFT BACK (ISBN 0 86157 002 2: 120 pps selected WAGBI approved recipes; menus; Cordon Bleu freezer section): £1.90

* **MISCELLANEOUS SMALL FORMAT BOOKS**

☐ EXPLORING HISTORIC CUMBRIA (ISBN 0 86157 005 7: 48 pps; 32 photographs): £1.25
☐ OVER THE SETTS (ISBN 0 86157 007 3: 48 pps; 43 vintage photographs of East Lancashire trams and buses in days gone by): £1.00
☐ WILLIAM FOGGITT'S WEATHER BOOK (ISBN 0 86157 012 X: 64 pps; 18 photographs; 7 line subjects; monthly weather lore): £1.00
☐ RIBBLE VALLEY RENDEZVOUS (ISBN 0 86157 011 1: 48 pps; 29 photographs; Where to Go; Where to Dine; What to See; An illustrated itinerary): £1.20

* MISCELLANEOUS SMALL FORMAT BOOKS (Continued)

☐ BARROW AT WAR (ISBN 0 86157 027 8: 48 pps): £1.20
☐ WINDOW ON WHALLEY (ISBN 0 86157 019 7: 32 pps; 14 photographs): £1.00

* **MEDIUM FORMAT (⅔ A4) BOOKS 'IN TIMES PAST' SERIES**

☐ STOURBRIDGE IN TIMES PAST (ISBN 0 86157 045 6): £2.00
☐ KIDDERMINSTER IN TIMES PAST (ISBN 0 86157 037 5): £1.80
☐ RUNCORN IN TIMES PAST (ISBN 0 86157 032 4): £1.80
☐ LANGBAURGH IN TIMES PAST (ISBN 0 86157 033 2): £1.80
☐ VINTAGE STOCKPORT (ISBN 0 86157 043 X): £2.00
☐ WALSINGHAM IN TIMES PAST (ISBN 0 86157 046 4): £2.00

* **OTHER COUNTRYSIDE PUBLICATIONS**

☐ NORTH WESTERN SAIL (Large A4 format: ISBN 0 86157 002 2: 56 pps; 112 photographs; from Whitehaven to Blackpool); £1.85
☐ NORTH WEST STEAMSHIPS ⅔ A4 FORMAT: £2.95
☐ SMILIN' THROUGH A5 FORMAT, LANCASHIRE DIALECT; SOFTBACK: £1.80; HARDBACK: £3.20

* **SPECIALITY BOOKS**

THE FATE OF THE LANCASHIRE WITCHES (ISBN 0 86157 001 4: small A5 format; 48 pps; 17 photographs; 8 interpretive line and wash drawings; witches' family tree; centre-spread map of Lancashire Witchways; four-colour front cover): £1.25 HARDBACK EDITION: £2.60

WILL THE REAL JACK THE RIPPER... (ISBN 0 86157 025 1: A5 format; 72 pps; photographs; interpretive line drawings; library map of murder sites; satirical cartoons; two-colour front cover): £1.60 HARDBACK EDITION: £2.60

Both publications available in cassette form (2 x 45 mins), specially read by Shakespearean actor William Maxwell.

All the above publications are in print, and should normally be available through your bookseller or larger newsagent. In case of difficulty, however, please direct your requirements to: **COUNTRYSIDE PUBLICATIONS LIMITED, SCHOOL LANE, BRINSCALL, Nr. CHORLEY, LANCASHIRE, ENGLAND,** remitting the stated amount by cheque or postal order.